SIMONE BILES

BY ANTHONY K. HEWSON

SportsZone

An Imprint of Abdo Publishing
abdobooks.com

abdobooks.com

Published by Abdo Publishing, a division of ABDO, PO Box 398166, Minneapolis, Minnesota
55439. Copyright © 2022 by Abdo Consulting Group, Inc. International copyrights reserved
in all countries. No part of this book may be reproduced in any form without written
permission from the publisher. SportsZone™ is a trademark and logo of Abdo Publishing.

Printed in the United States of America, North Mankato, Minnesota.
102021
012022

THIS BOOK CONTAINS
RECYCLED MATERIALS

Cover Photo: Ashley Landis/AP Images
Interior Photos: Rebecca Blackwell/AP Images, 4-5, 22-23; Dmitri Lovetsky/AP Images,
6; Kyodo/AP Images, 7, 24; Mike Blake/Reuters/Newscom, 8-9; Shutterstock Images,
10; Matthias Schrader/AP Images, 11, 20-21; Thomas Eisenhuth/picture-alliance/dpa/AP
Images, 12-13; Yves Logghe/AP Images, 14-15; Elise Amendola/AP Images, 16-17; Andy
Wong/AP Images, 18, 19; Marijan Murat/dpa/AP Images, 25; AJ Mast/AP Images, 26; Eric
Risberg/AP Images, 27; David McIntyre/Zuma Press Wire/AP Images, 28-29

Editor: Chrös McDougall
Series Designer: Jake Nordby

Library of Congress Control Number: 2021945010

Publisher's Cataloging-in-Publication Data

Names: Hewson, Anthony K., author.
Title: Simone Biles / by Anthony K. Hewson
Description: Minneapolis, Minnesota : Abdo Publishing, 2022 | Series: Olympic stars set 3 |
      Includes online resources and index.
Identifiers: ISBN 9781532197390 (lib. bdg.) | ISBN 9781644947562 (pbk.) | ISBN
      9781098219628 (ebook)
Subjects: LCSH: Biles, Simone, 1997---Juvenile literature. | Gymnastics--Juvenile
      literature. | Women gymnasts--Juvenile literature. | Women Olympic athletes--
      Juvenile literature. | African American women--Juvenile literature. | Athletes, Black-
      -Juvenile literature.
Classification: DDC 796.44092--dc23

CONTENTS

OLYMPIC GOLD **4**

TOUGH BEGINNINGS **8**

ROAD TO THE TOP **14**

THE GOAT **22**

TIMELINE 30
GLOSSARY 31
INDEX 32
ONLINE RESOURCES 32
ABOUT THE AUTHOR 32

Simone Biles performs on the balance beam in the all-around final at the 2016 Olympics.

OLYMPIC GOLD

US gymnast Simone Biles had work to do. The individual all-around competition at the 2016 Olympic Games was half over, and Biles trailed Russia's Aliya Mustafina. Then Biles wobbled on the balance beam. It was a situation nobody expected for Biles. She was the three-time defending world champion. Many assumed she would cruise to a gold medal.

But then Mustafina struggled even more on beam. Biles took over first place. Only the floor exercise remained.

Biles was nearly flawless on the floor. The 19-year-old opened with a full-twisting double layout. It was the beginning of a series of dizzying flips and spins. Each tumbling pass was more impressive than the one that came before it. Ninety seconds later, there was no doubt. Biles was the winner.

Her tears flowed as she realized that she had achieved her dream. "Every emotion hit me at once so I was just kind of a train wreck," she said. But Biles had no time to rest. More Olympic gold would soon follow.

Biles, *left*, and US teammate Aly Raisman celebrate after Biles won gold and Raisman won silver in the Olympic all-around final.

Biles leaps into the air during the floor exercise final in the 2016 Olympics.

FAST FACT

Biles won the all-around gold medal by 2.1 points. It was the largest margin of victory in the Olympics since new scoring went into effect in 2008.

TOUGH BEGINNINGS

Simone Arianne Biles was born on March 14, 1997, in Columbus, Ohio. Life started out tough for Simone. Her mother, Shanon, struggled with drug addiction. When Simone was three years old, Shanon gave up Simone and her three siblings. Simone's grandfather and his wife, Ronald and Nellie Biles, adopted Simone in 2003. They also adopted her younger sister, Adria.

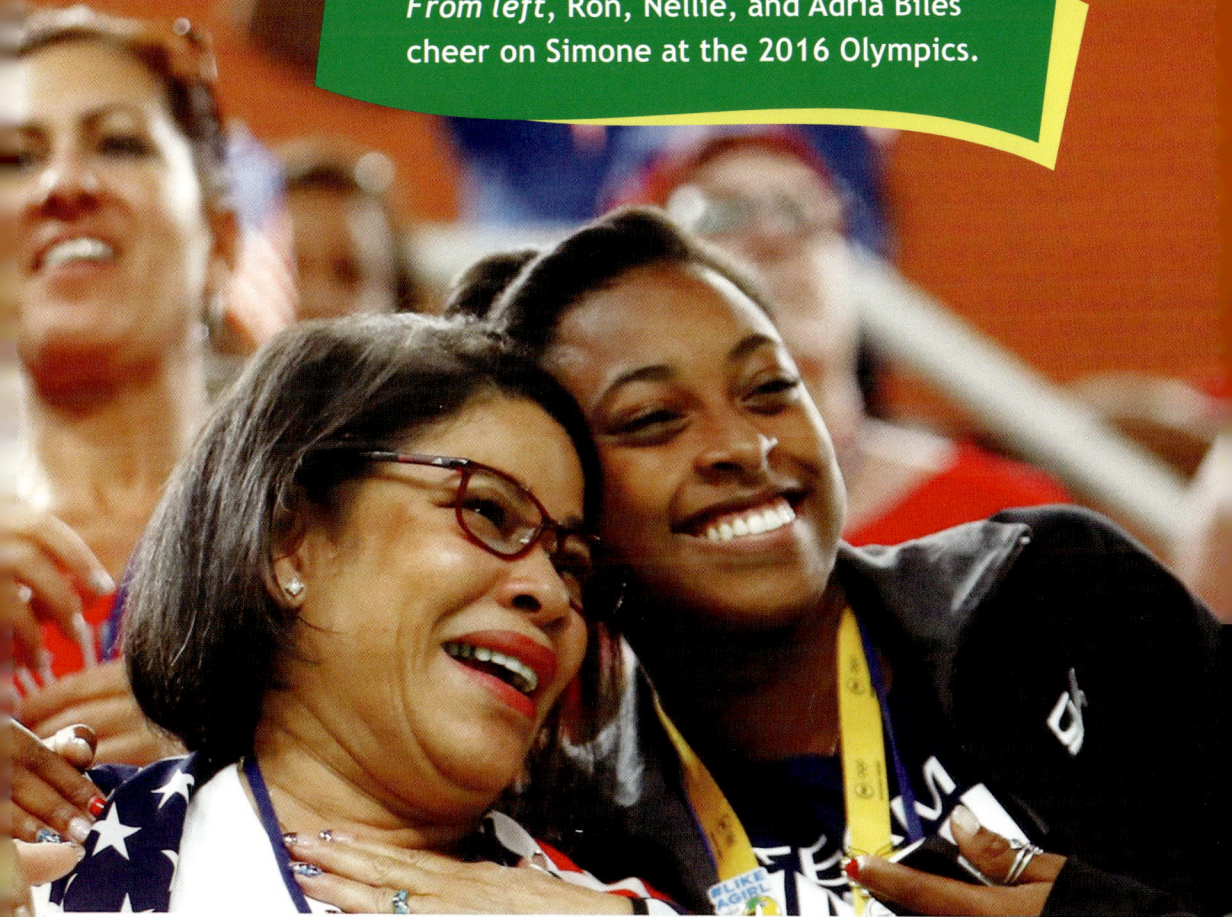

9

Simone and her sister moved to an area just outside of Houston, Texas. When Simone was six years old, she visited a gymnastics center. The trip changed her life. Simone watched the gymnasts doing flips and twists. She signed up and began her training. Simone's athletic ability made her a natural gymnast. Soon after, she began working with a young coach named Aimee Boorman. They proved to be a perfect match.

Simone and her sister moved to the Houston, Texas, area in 2003.

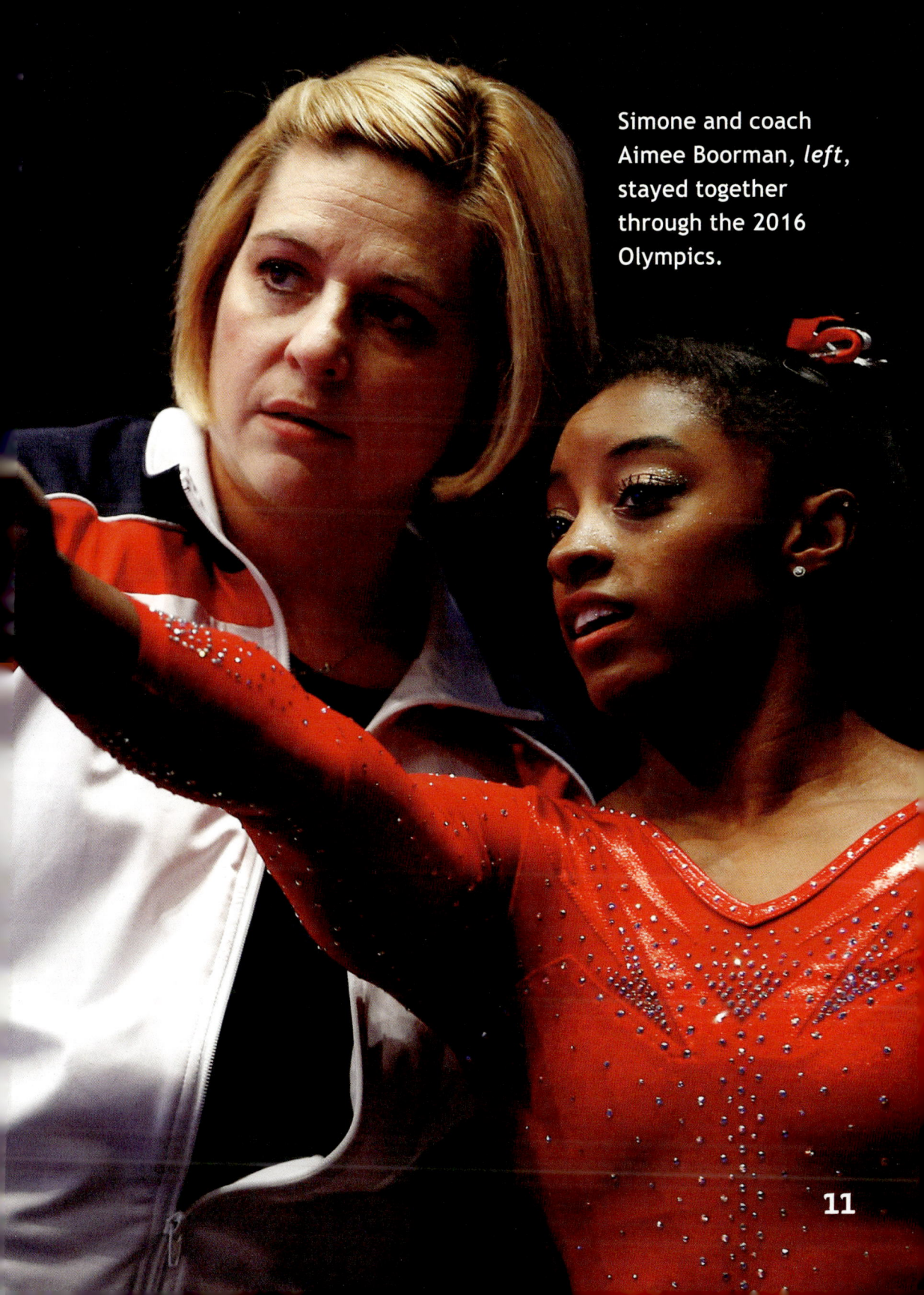

Simone and coach Aimee Boorman, *left*, stayed together through the 2016 Olympics.

FAST FACT

Simone trained for around 20 hours per week while she was in public school. Homeschooling allowed her to increase her training to 32 hours per week.

Simone had talent. But early on, she did not look like the world's best gymnast. Some observers said she lacked flexibility. In 2012 Biles started homeschooling. That gave her more time for training. The extra work paid off. By 2013, at age 16, Biles was ready to step up to the senior level. She was about to take on the best gymnasts in the world.

ROAD TO THE TOP

One of Simone Biles's first senior events was the 2013 US Classic. It was a disaster. She fell in each of her first three events. Her performance was so bad that her coach pulled her from the competition.

"Nothing was really going right," Biles explained later. "I guess I just wasn't in a very good mental place."

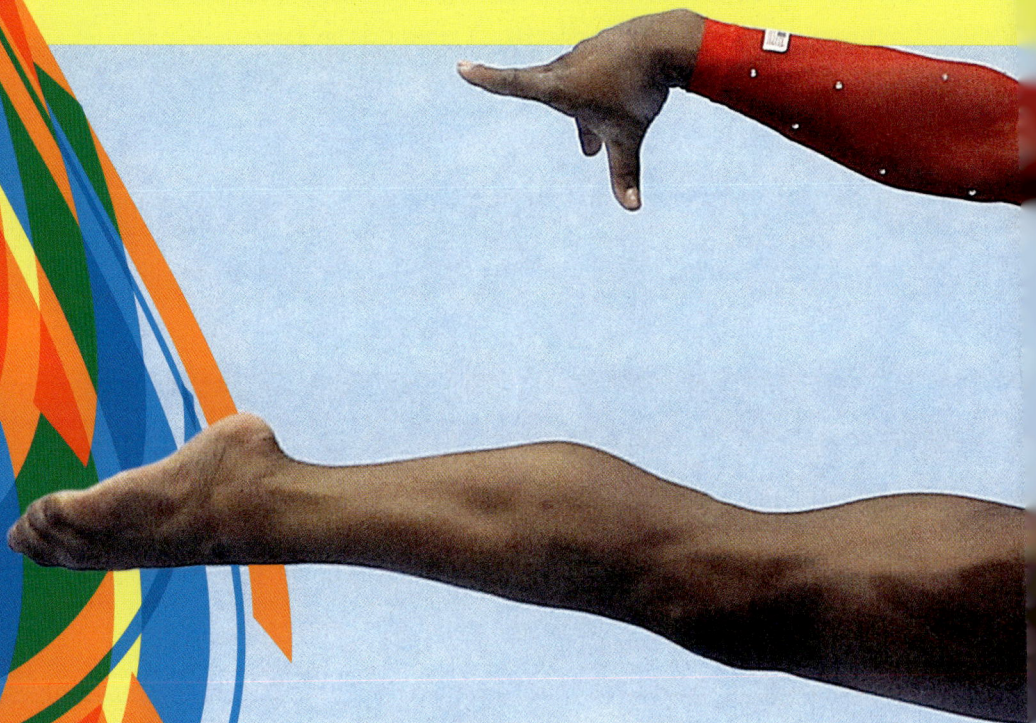

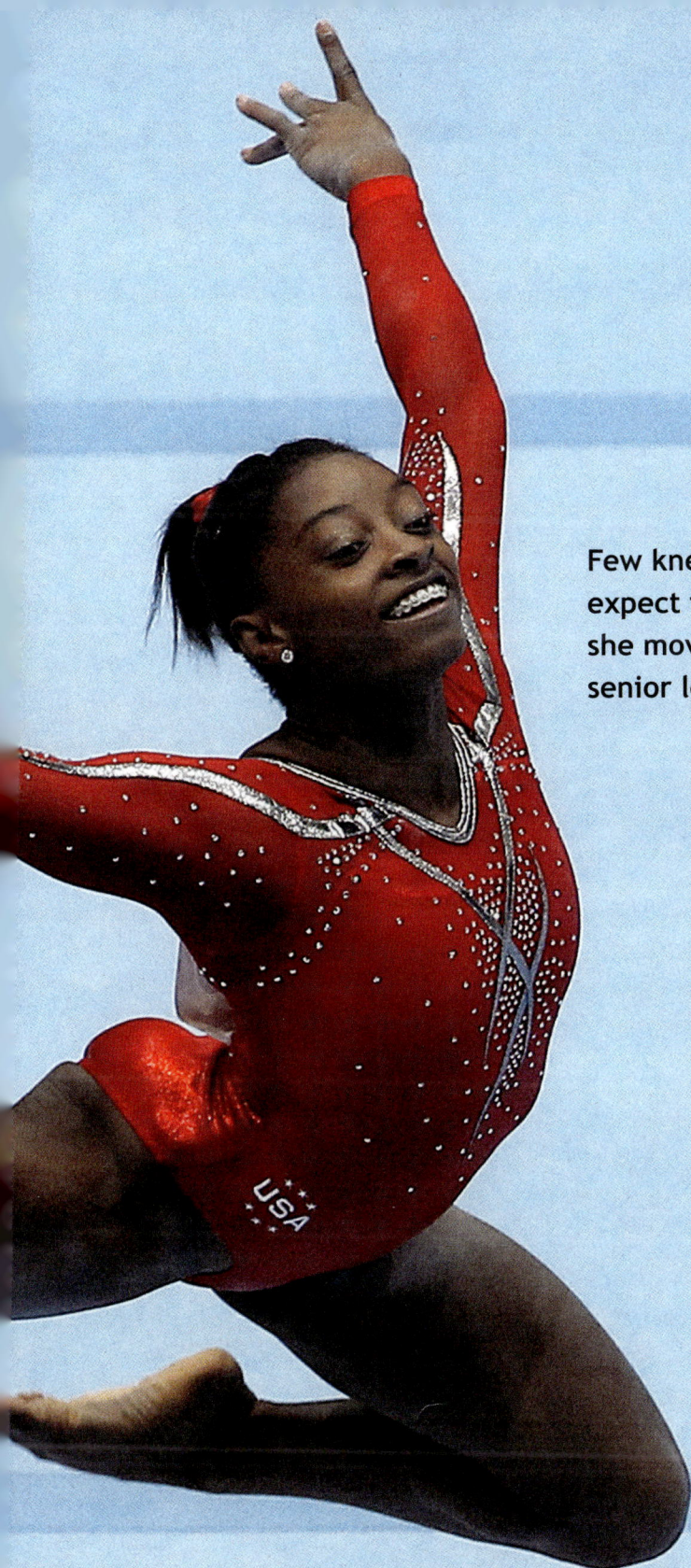

Few knew what to expect from Biles when she moved up to the senior level in 2013.

Biles worked to improve her focus. Less than a month later, she won the US all-around title. Fans were amazed by her difficult routines. Her power allowed her to do things that few other gymnasts could even try. And she performed them with near perfect technique, too. Her skills were on display six weeks later at the 2013 World Championships. Biles won the all-around title by almost a full point.

Biles showed more consistency at the 2013 US championships.

Biles lights up the floor exercise at the 2014 World Championships.

FAST FACT

Biles is scared of insects. At the 2014 World Championships, she darted off the podium when she saw a bee in her flowers!

Biles kept winning and winning—and winning. Many gymnasts excel on one or two apparatuses while struggling in others. But Biles was among the world's best in all four. She won world titles in floor exercise and balance beam. Her vault and uneven bars performances were among the best in the world, too. That versatility made her unstoppable in the all-around event. She was winning every one she entered. And the scores were not even close to those of her competitors.

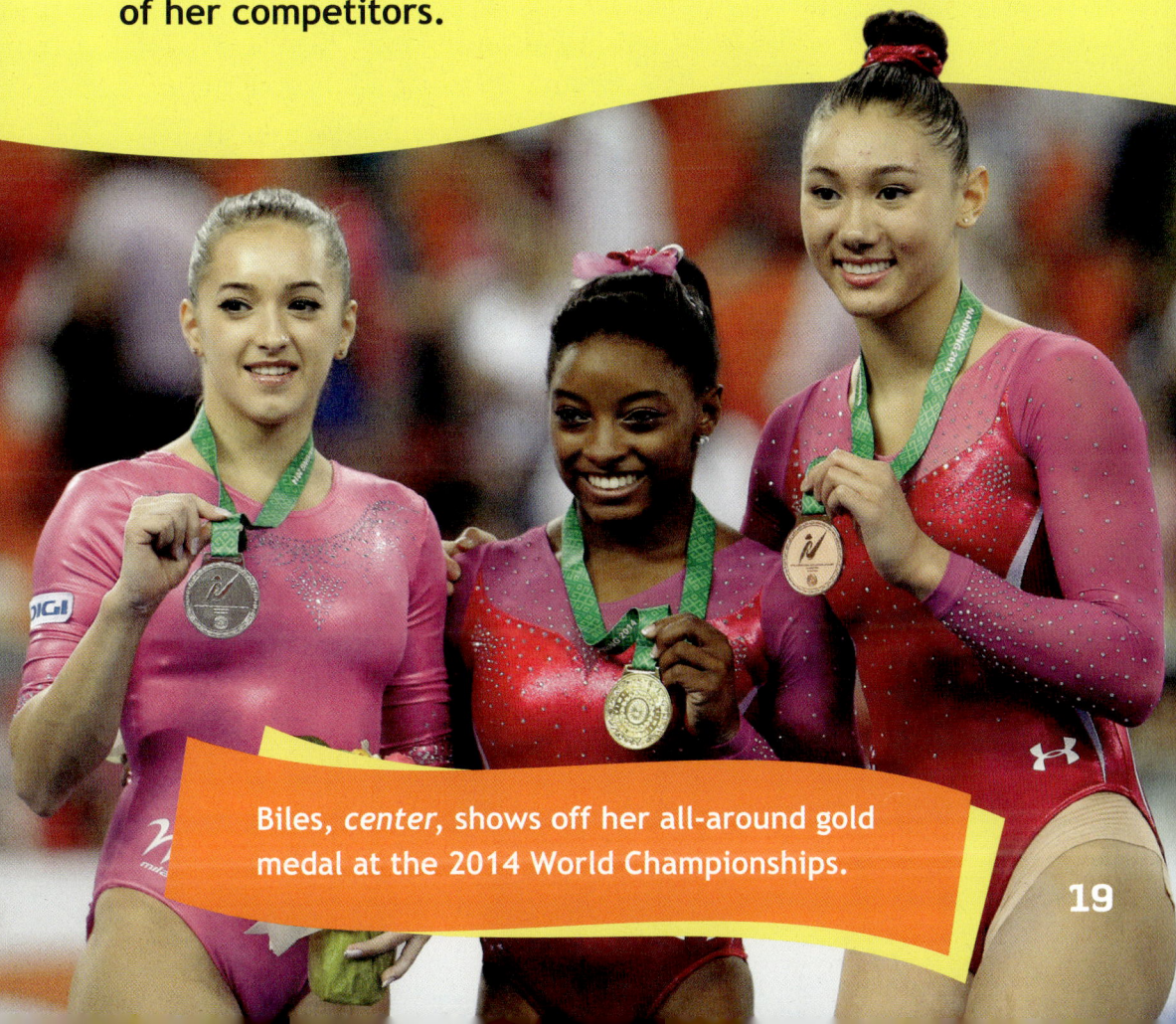

Biles, *center*, shows off her all-around gold medal at the 2014 World Championships.

Biles performs on the balance beam at the 2015 World Championships.

Biles won all-around gold again at the 2015 Worlds. This time she beat her teammate and the reigning Olympic champ, Gabby Douglas. Biles totaled four gold medals and one bronze at the event. It gave her a career total of 14 medals. That is the most in the history of women's gymnastics. She was so much better than everyone else that her teammates joked they were competing for second place.

FAST FACT
Biles was chosen to carry the US flag in the closing ceremony of the 2016 Olympic Games.

THE GOAT

Simone Biles was the best in the world by a wide margin. Just one thing remained: Olympic glory. The 2016 Olympic Games were held in Rio de Janeiro, Brazil.

Team USA was favored to win gold in Rio. And Biles was favored to star individually. She and her teammates began by winning team gold. Biles easily won the all-around. She also scored gold on vault and the floor exercise, plus bronze on the balance beam. With four gold medals, Biles tied the record for the most at one Olympics by a female gymnast.

Biles amazed viewers around the world with her performance at the 2016 Olympics in Rio.

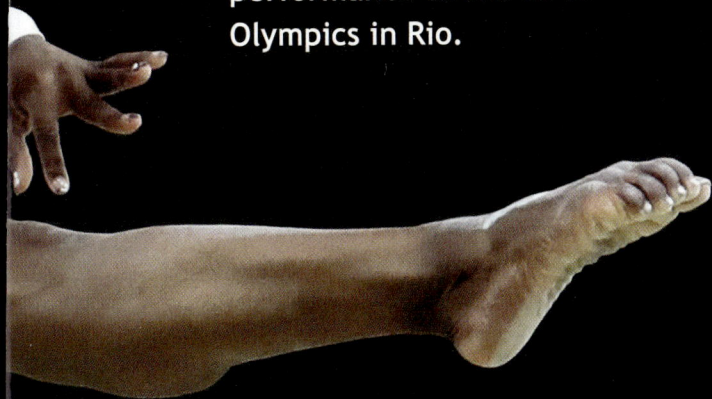

Biles took a year off from competing in 2017. She picked up right where she left off in 2018. Biles won medals in all six events at the 2018 World Championships. Four of them were golds.

The next year, Biles won five more gold medals at the 2019 World Championships, bringing her total to 25. With those she broke the record for most Worlds medals of any gymnast, male or female. She also set a record for the most gold medals, with 19. People began calling Biles the "GOAT," meaning greatest of all time.

A composite image shows Biles's impressive performance on the vault at the 2019 World Championships.

Biles shows the amazing five gold medals she won at the 2019 World Championships.

FAST FACT

Gymnasts are scored based on difficulty and execution. The best possible execution score is 10. With a 6.6 difficulty score and a 9.5 execution score, Biles's historic vault earned her a 16.1.

No woman had performed a Yurchenko double pike vault until Biles did so at the 2021 US Classic.

Biles was all set to defend her Olympic medals at the 2020 Games in Tokyo, Japan. But the COVID-19 pandemic delayed the Olympics by a year. At the US Classic in May 2021, she performed a vault with a difficulty score of 6.6. That made it the most difficult vault ever completed by a female gymnast.

Heading into Tokyo, Biles hadn't lost an all-around competition she had entered since 2013. She was the gold-medal favorite again.

Airline workers gave Biles a warm send-off as she prepared to leave for Tokyo.

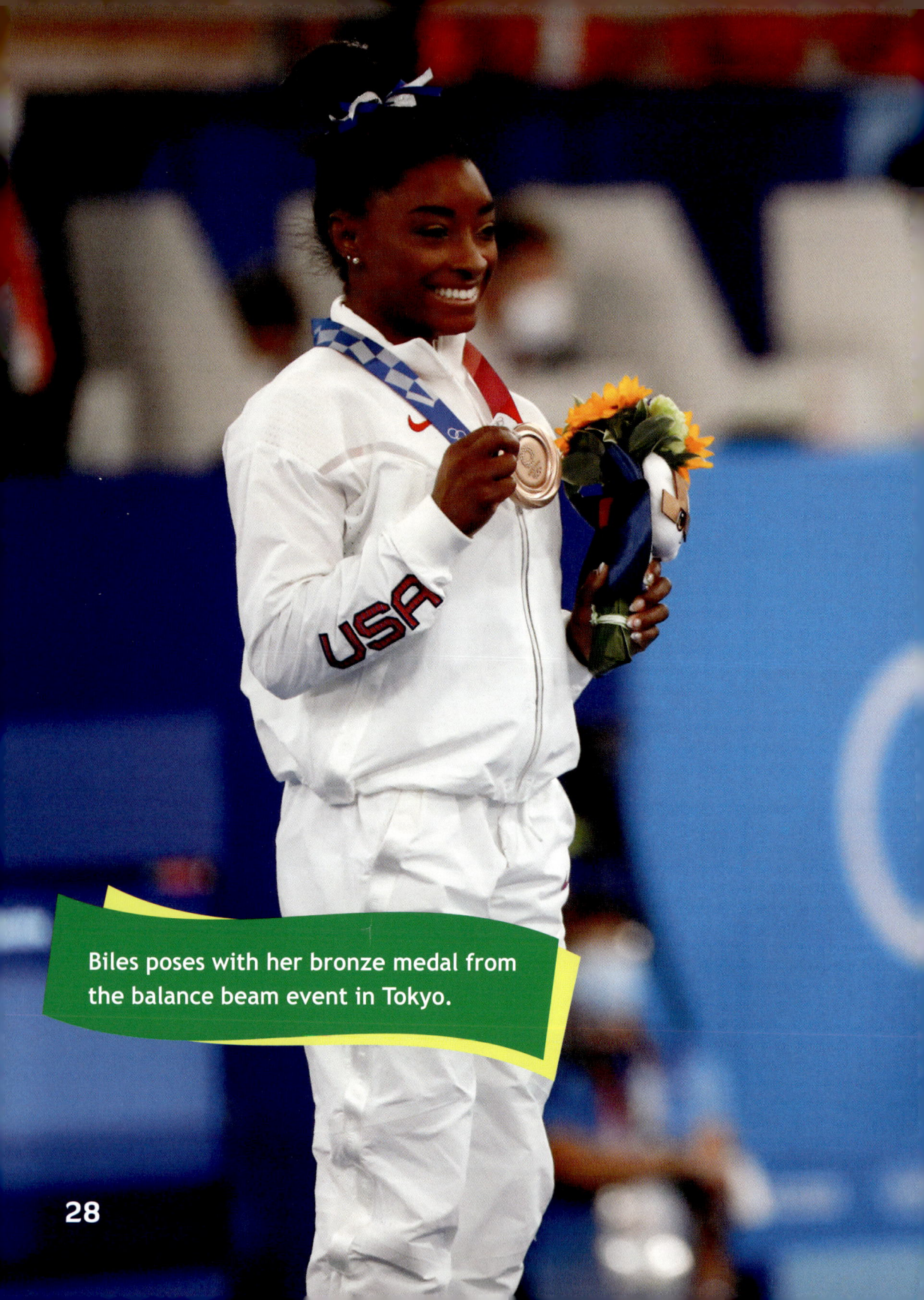

Biles poses with her bronze medal from the balance beam event in Tokyo.

Biles helped her team win silver to open the competition. But she wasn't able to finish the team event. She was feeling disoriented in the air. She later withdrew from the all-around and all but one individual event final. That was the balance beam. Biles finished the Tokyo Games on a high note by winning a bronze medal in the event.

It wasn't what she expected. But Biles said the bronze meant more than gold. It showed how she battled through challenges. And it was yet another medal for one of the greatest of all time.

FAST FACT

Gymnasts who perform a new skill at a major competition get that skill named for them. Biles has one skill named after her on vault, one on balance beam, and two on floor exercise.

TIMELINE

1997
Simone Arianne Biles is born on March 14 in Columbus, Ohio.

2003
Simone and her younger sister, Adria, are adopted by their grandfather and his wife, Ronald and Nellie Biles.

2012
Biles begins homeschooling so that she can spend more time practicing in the gym.

2013
Biles wins the all-around and floor exercise in her debut at the World Championships.

2015
Biles wins her third straight all-around gold at the World Championships.

2016
Biles dominates at the 2016 Olympics in Brazil, winning four gold medals and one bronze.

2018
After a break from the sport, Biles wins six medals (four of them gold) at the World Championships.

2019
Biles sets a new record with her 25th World Championships medal. She also has a record 19 world titles.

2021
Biles qualifies for all five individual event finals at the Olympics in Japan but withdraws from four of them. Biles wins a team silver medal and a bronze on balance beam.

GLOSSARY

addiction
A dependence on a substance such as drugs or alcohol.

adopt
To legally take in somebody else's child as your own.

all-around
A gymnastics competition in which women compete in all four events.

apparatus
One of four pieces of equipment in women's gymnastics: balance beam, floor exercise, uneven bars, and vault.

execution
The ability to properly complete a gymnastics routine.

favorite
The person or team expected to win.

flexibility
The degree to which a person can bend and move her or his body.

homeschooling
When a student takes classes at home instead of going to a school.

margin
The difference between two things.

routine
A set performance by a gymnast in one event.

senior
An elite gymnast who is 16 or older in a given year.

tumbling pass
A series in which a gymnast connects multiple gymnastics elements, such as flips and handsprings.

INDEX

Biles, Adria, 8, 10
Biles, Nellie, 8
Biles, Ronald, 8
Boorman, Aimee, 10

Columbus, Ohio, 8
COVID-19 pandemic, 27

Douglas, Gabby, 21

homeschooling, 12, 13
Houston, Texas, 10

medals, 5, 7, 21, 23, 24, 27, 29
Mustafina, Aliya, 5

Olympic Games (Rio de Janeiro), 5-6, 7, 22, 23
Olympic Games (Tokyo), 27, 29

records, 7, 21, 23, 24, 26, 27

Spring, Texas, 20

US Classic, 14, 26, 27

World Champions Centre, 20
World Championships, 16, 18, 24

Online Resources

Booklinks
NONFICTION NETWORK
FREE! ONLINE NONFICTION RESOURCES

To learn more about Simone Biles, please visit **abdobooklinks.com** or scan this QR code. These links are routinely monitored and updated to provide the most current information available.

About the Author

Anthony K. Hewson is a freelance writer originally from San Diego. He and his wife now live in the San Francisco Bay Area with their two dogs.